THE JEWISH CHILDREN'S BIBLE
NUMBERS

Adapted by Sheryl Prenzlau

PITSPOPANY

NEW YORK ▾ JERUSALEM

God sent a strong wind that blew quail to the camp of Israel.

Published by Pitspopany Press
Text copyright © 1998 by Sheryl Prenzlau
Illustrations copyright © 1998 by Zely Smekhov

Design: Benjie Herskowitz

PITSPOPANY PRESS books may be purchased for educational or special sales by contacting:
Marketing Director, Pitspopany Press, 40 East 78th Street, New York, New York 10021.
Fax: 212 472-6253.

ISBN: 0-943706-34-3

Printed in Hungary

Contents

Continued on next page

Contents

Continued from previous page

Counting The People   במדבר

wo years and two months after the Israelites left Egypt, God told Moses to count the people. Every man from the age of 20 (the age when men went into the army) was counted. The princes of the Twelve Tribes helped Moses and his brother, Aaron, count the people.

The total number of male Israelites counted was 603,550.

But the Tribe of Levi was counted separately.

Choosing The Levites

God told Moses to separate the Tribe of Levi from the other tribes. They had special work to do for God. But first, the Children of Israel put their hands on the Levites to show that the Levites were their representatives to God. Then Aaron and Moses lifted up each Levite to show that the Levites were going to help the Kohanim and the people.

Finally, the Levites put their hands on two animals. These animals would be sacrificed to God.

Counting The Levites

The Levites were in charge of the mishkan – the house of God – and everything that was in it. They set up their tents around the mishkan. When the Children of Israel traveled, the Levites took apart the mishkan. They used poles to carry many of the vessels on their shoulders. When the Israelites rested, the Levites put the mishkan back together again.

There were three families in the Tribe of Levi. Each family was named after one of the sons of Levi: Gershon, Kehat, and Merari.

God told Moses to count the members of each family. Moses was to count the Levite boys who were one month or older. The total number of Levites counted was 22,000.

God told Moses that the Levites were to work with the Kohanim in the mishkan, from the age of 25 until they reached the age of 50. They were also to sing and play music in the mishkan. From 50 years and older they stopped working in the mishkan.

Levites And The Firstborn Israelites

God saved the Jewish firstborn during the last plague in Egypt, so the firstborn were supposed to work for God. But, because the firstborn sinned by worshipping the Golden Calf, God chose the Levites to work in the mishkan instead.

There were 22,000 Levites and 22,273 firstborn. Since there were no Levites to change places with the extra 273 firstborn, each firstborn brought five shekels of money to Aaron the Kohen and his sons. Since there was no Levite to take the place of these 273 firstborn, the money took the place of these firstborn and was used in the mishkan.

Today, many parents give five shekels worth of money to a Kohen when they have a firstborn boy. This is called *Pidyan Habain,* exchanging the son.

THE SOTAH

נשא

A Sotah is a married woman who doesn't seem to love her husband anymore. Her husband sees her with another man, and gets angry.

God said that if a man thinks that his wife doesn't love him anymore he should tell her to stop seeing the other man. If she refuses, then he must bring her to the Kohen Gadol.

The Kohen Gadol is to give the woman a certain drink. If her husband is right, and she really doesn't love him and loves someone else, then the drink will be very bitter, and everyone will know she did a terrible thing. But if her husband is wrong, then the waters will turn sweet, and she will feel wonderful.

THE NAZIR

A Nazir is someone who promises that for a certain amount of time – thirty days or more – he will try to get closer to God. He promises not to drink wine, not to cut his hair, and not to touch a dead body, not even if he is asked to help bury a relative.

When the time of the Nazir's promise is over, he cuts his hair and brings sacrifices. Then he can drink wine and be like everyone else again.

Aaron Blesses The People

God told Moses to tell Aaron and his sons to bless the Children of Israel. If they do this, God will bless the people too.
Here is the blessing Aaron is to give the people:

May God bless you and keep you safe.
May God's presence shine on you and may you find
favor in God's eyes.
May God's presence turn to you and bring you peace.

The Mishkan Is Completed

When Moses completed the mishkan, the Princes of the Tribes brought presents for the mishkan. These presents were given by Moses to the Levites to be used for the mishkan. The Princes also brought sacrifices.

Then Moses came to the *Ohel Moed*, the place where God's presence lived. He heard the voice of God speaking to him from the top of the cover of the Ark. The Voice came from between the two angelic *Cherubim* that were on the Ark.

Lighting The Menorah בהעלותך

God commanded Moses to tell Aaron to make sure that the lamps of the menorah were all facing toward the middle. When Aaron lit them, he made sure they all faced toward the middle of the menorah.

The menorah itself was made of pure gold from top to bottom.

The Second Passover

One year after the Children of Israel left Egypt, in the month of Nissan, God commanded everyone to make the Passover sacrifice, even though they were in the desert.

However, there were people who couldn't make the Passover sacrifice because they had come into contact with a dead body. They wanted to celebrate Passover, too. So God said, "If someone can't make the Passover sacrifice in the month of Nissan, then he can make the Passover sacrifice a month later, in the month of Iyyar. But everyone must make the Passover sacrifice with matzah and bitter herbs, or they will be committing a great sin."

Travel In The Desert

The Children of Israel traveled through the desert by following the pillar of cloud that appeared on the mishkan during the day and the pillar of fire that appeared at night. Sometimes the cloud remained on the mishkan for a short time, and when it started to move, everyone followed. Sometimes the cloud rested on the mishkan for a long time, and then everyone stayed in one place.

Blowing The Trumpets

God told Moses to make two trumpets. The Kohanim were the ones who blew the trumpets. The sounds that they made could mean many different things. If the people had to gather together, the Kohanim blew a long blast on the trumpets. A short blast on the trumpets meant it was time to move on. Many short blasts meant that the people had to go to war to fight their enemies. On Holy Days the trumpets were sounded, too.

The Order Of Travel

There was an order to the way the Children of Israel traveled through the desert.

First, the Tribe of **Judah** began to leave, followed by the Tribes of **Issachar** and **Zevulun**.

Then the mishkan was taken down by two of the families of the Levites, **Gershon** and **Merari**.

The Tribe of **Reuven** rose, followed by the Tribes of **Shimon** and **Gad**.

Then the third family of Levites, **Kehat,** carried the mishkan.

The Tribe of **Ephraim** went, followed by the Tribes of **Menashe** and **Binyamin.**

Finally, the Tribe of **Dan** began to leave, and the Tribes of **Asher** and **Naftali** followed.

A Special Prayer

When the Ark was about to be carried, Moses said, *"Arise God, and make all Your enemies scatter before You."* When the Ark rested, Moses said, *"Return God, to the many thousands of the Children of Israel."*

The Complainers

There were those in the desert who began to complain.

"Who will feed us meat?" they asked. And everyone joined in, saying, "Who will feed us meat?"

They remembered the foods they had eaten in Egypt and were

hungry for these foods. "But now we have nothing," they complained, "except the manna."

Moses was angry. Everyone knew that the manna was beautiful to look at, very tasty, and easy to find. But they continued to complain.

"What do you want from me?" Moses asked God. "Can I give meat to all these people? It's too much for me!"

God told him to tell the people, "You want meat? You'll get meat! Not for one day or two days, but for 30 days! Until the meat comes out of your nose, and you can't look at it anymore!"

Quail

God sent a strong wind that blew quail from the sea to the camp of Israel. The people got up in the morning and saw the quail. They gathered it all that day and the next day. There were quail everywhere, and everyone was eating quail.

Then, when they were stuffed with quail, those who had demanded meat and didn't believe in God, died.

Seventy Wise Men

God told Moses to gather 70 wise men to help him deal with the people and answer their questions. When these people were gathered together, God made them even wiser so they could help Moses.

Two men, Eldad and Medad, became prophets and began to tell the future to the people around them. Someone ran over to Moses and told him what was happening.

Joshua, Moses' helper, was angry that other people were acting like they knew more than Moses, and he wanted the two men locked up.

"Don't be jealous on my account," Moses told Joshua. "I wish everyone could be a prophet."

Miriam Gets Punished

Miriam and Aaron said things that weren't nice about Moses, their brother. They felt that even though God spoke to Moses, Moses shouldn't think that he was so great. After all, God spoke to them too.

The truth was that Moses was the most humble man in the world. He didn't think for a moment that he was great.

God was angry with Miriam and Aaron because of what they said.

He told them that all the prophets in the world hear God through a dream, but to Moses alone God talks "mouth to mouth."

"Why did you not fear to speak against My servant Moses?" God asked them.

Then the cloud that was on the mishkan rose, and Miriam's skin became white as snow, a sign that she had the disease, *tzaraas*.

Aaron saw this and cried to Moses to help her. He was afraid she would die.

"Please heal her now, God," Moses prayed.

God said to Moses, "If her father was angry with her, wouldn't she hide her face? Let her go outside the camp of Israel for seven days, and then she will be cured."

The Children of Israel waited seven days until Miriam was healed, and then they moved onward.

Moses Sends Spies Into The Land Of Canaan שלח

In those days the Land of Israel was called Canaan. Moses sent 12 spies to see if Canaan would be difficult or easy to conquer. The 12 men he sent were heads of the Twelve Tribes of Israel.

Moses told the 12 spies to check out the people in the land, to see if they were strong and mighty; to look through the land, to see if it was good or bad; and to spy on the cities, to see if they had high walls surrounding them or no walls at all.

The 12 spies were supposed to bring back samples of any fruit they found in the land.

The Spies Return

For 40 days the spies wandered through the land of Canaan. They returned with pomegranates, figs, and a giant cluster of grapes.

They told Moses and the people that "the land flows with milk and honey, and this is the fruit we found. But the people in the land are very powerful, and their cities have big walls around them. Some of the people who live in the land are giants, and we were like grasshoppers to them. We can't go into this land!"

But two of the 12 spies – Joshua, the leader of the Tribe of Ephraim, and Calev, the leader of the Tribe of Judah – cried out, "Don't listen to the others. The land is very, very good! God is with us!"

Instead of listening to Joshua and Calev, the Children of Israel wanted to throw stones at them and run back to Egypt.

But, suddenly, God's presence was seen in the mishkan.

Forty Years Of Wandering

God said to Moses, "How long will these people continue to rebel? How long will they continue to distrust Me despite everything I do for them? Moses, I will destroy them all and make your children into a great nation instead!"

But Moses didn't want this to happen. He pleaded with God, saying, "If You kill all Your people, the nations of the world will say that God was not able to bring this people into the land of their forefathers. They will say You could not keep Your promise."

Moses begged God to forgive the people.

God agreed not to kill all the people. But they would not be permitted to enter the land of Canaan. Instead, for every one of the 40 days that the spies were in Canaan, the people would have to wander one full year in the desert. For 40 years they would wander through the desert until the whole generation was no longer alive. Only Joshua and Calev would enter the Land with the new generation of Israelites.

The Mitzvah Of Challah

God told Moses that when the Children of Israel finally enter the Land and bake bread, they must be careful to take off a portion of the dough and set it aside for God. This is the mitzvah of *Challah*.

The Convert

Moses taught the people many laws, but he repeated, over and over again, this very important rule. The same laws that apply to the Children of Israel also apply to anyone who decides to convert and become part of the Jewish people. No one is permitted to treat a convert differently than someone who is born Jewish.

Rebelling Against The Shabbat

One Shabbat the people saw a man gathering wood. This was strictly forbidden on Shabbat, but the man did not care. No one had ever done something like this on Shabbat before, so Moses and Aaron didn't know what to do with him.

They decided to put the man in jail, and then Moses prayed to God, asking what to do. God told Moses that the man had to die for rebelling against God and the Shabbat.

The man was brought outside the camp of Israel, and there he was stoned by the people.

The Law Of Tzitzit

God told Moses to tell the people to make tzitzit on the corners of their garments. This was to be a commandment for all generations.

"You must tie a special blue thread called *techaylet* with each tzitzit," God commanded. "And when you look at the tzitzit you should remember who you are and that I give you commandments to make you holy. I am the God who took you out of Egypt. I am your God."

Korach Challenges Moses And Aaron קרח

Korach was from the Tribe of Levi. He convinced more than 250 famous men from among the people to go with him to complain to Moses and Aaron.

"You have taken on too much for yourselves!" they said to Moses and Aaron. "God is with all of us. We don't need you to lead us."

Moses heard this and felt terrible.

"We'll let God decide who will be the leaders," Moses said. "Tomorrow, you and your people take incense pans and put incense in them and then put fire in them. The person whose incense God chooses will be the leader."

Then Moses told Korach that it was wrong for him to want to take Aaron's job as well. Being a Levite should be enough for him. "Why do you want to be a Kohen too?" Moses asked.

A Giant Mouth

The next day Korach and all his followers took the incense pans, put incense and fire in them, and waited in front of the mishkan, together with Moses and Aaron.

God told Moses to move all the people far away from Korach. The people did as they were told.

Then Moses said, "Now you will all know that God sent me to

lead you. I didn't ask to be the leader. If these people die a normal death, then I am not God's chosen leader. But if the earth opens up its mouth and swallows them all, then you know that God has chosen me, and they have rebelled against God."

Sure enough, when Moses finished speaking, the ground opened up like a mouth and swallowed Korach. Then God sent a flame which destroyed the men who were offering the incense.

The Flowering Staff

Next, God told Moses to gather the staffs of each of the leaders of the Twelve Tribes. Every leader was to carve his name on his staff. The name of Aaron was carved on the staff of Levi.

The staffs were collected and put in front of the Ark in the mishkan. The one whose staff blossomed with a flower would be the chosen Kohen of God.

Moses put all the staffs in front of the Ark. The next day everyone saw that the staff of Aaron had blossomed. Not only that, but it had sprouted a bud, and ripe almonds were on the staff.

God told Moses to take Aaron's staff and leave it in front of the Ark so that everyone would remember whom God had chosen to be the Kohen. This way the people would stop complaining.

The Kohanim And Levites

Aaron was told by God that the job of the Kohanim was to offer all the sacrifices of the people to God. In return, the people were to bring the Kohanim *terumah*, gifts of food. The Kohanim were to get the best oil, wine and grain, as well as the first fruits of the Land.

But the Kohanim were not to have a portion of the Land of Israel. God would be their portion. God would take care of them.

The Levites were to be in charge of the mishkan and everything in it. For doing this work for God, the Levites would receive *ma'aser*, a tenth of the crops of every field. They too would not own land because, like the Kohanim, they were separated from the people and could only work for God.

The Red Cow
חקת

The Children of Israel were told to take a completely red cow and give it to Elazar, Aaron's son. This red cow could not have any mark on it or anything wrong with it. No work could be done with it.

Elazar was to take the cow out of the camp where it would be burned and its ashes put aside for safekeeping. The ashes were needed because, if a person touched a dead human body, he had to leave the camp of Israel. He could only return when water mixed with the ashes of the red cow was sprinkled on him.

The Sin Of Moses

The Children of Israel had been wandering a long time until they came to a desert called Zin. There, Miriam, the sister of Moses, died. Right afterwards, the people ran out of water. They gathered around Moses and Aaron and began to complain.

"Why did you take us out of Egypt just to die in the desert?" they cried. "There's nothing here. No food, and no water to drink!"

God appeared to Moses and Aaron.

"Take your staff, Moses," God said, "and bring everyone to that rock over there. Speak to the rock, and it will pour out water for everyone, even their animals."

Moses did as God commanded. He brought the people to the rock, but he was so angry with them that instead of talking to the rock, Moses hit the rock, twice. A stream of water poured out of the rock, enough water for everyone and their animals.

But God was not happy with what Moses did. God said, "The people were supposed to see you talking to the rock before the water poured out. But you did not obey my instructions, and you hit the rock. For this, you will be punished. You will not bring my people into the Land of Israel."

The Land Of Edom

In order to get to the Land of Israel, Moses had to take the people through the land of Edom. He sent messengers to the king of Edom, asking permission to cross his land.

"If you let us cross your land," the messengers told the king, "we promise not to bother anyone. We won't even drink the water in your wells."

But the king of Edom refused. He gathered a large army and threatened to attack, unless the Children of Israel went around his land.

Aaron Dies

Moses led the people to a mountain called Hor, which was on the border of Edom.

God said to Moses and Aaron, "On this mountain Aaron will die."

Moses took Aaron and Elazar, Aaron's son, up the mountain. There, Moses took the special Kohen Gadol clothing that had been Aaron's and put it on Elazar. Elazar would now be the Kohen Gadol.

Then Aaron died on the mountain.

When the people saw that Aaron did not come down the mountain, they understood that he had died, and they cried for 30 days.

Snake Attack

As they traveled around the land of Edom, the people began to complain again.

"Why did you bring us out of Egypt only to die in the desert?" they asked angrily. "There is no food or water here, and we're fed up with this manna!"

God sent poisonous snakes to attack the people.

"We have sinned!" they cried, when the snakes entered the camp.

"We have sinned against God and you," the people admitted to Moses. "Pray to God to get rid of the snakes."

Moses prayed to God, and God told him to make a snake of copper and place it on a pole. When a person who was bitten by a snake looked at the snake on the pole, he was healed and lived.

The Battles Against Sihon And Og

Moses sent messengers to Sihon, king of the Amorite nation. Just as he had asked the King of Edom, he now asked Sihon to allow them to pass through his land. But like the King of Edon, Sihon also said no.

Sihon sent his mighty army out to fight the Children of Israel. But this time the Children of Israel fought back. God helped them, and they destroyed Sihon and the Amorite army. The Children of Israel took over the cities of the Amorites and settled in them.

Then Og, king of Bashan, which was also part of the Amorite land, came out to fight Moses and the people. Og was a giant, but God told Moses that Og would fall just like Sihon did, and that's just what happened. Og and all his people were destroyed, and the Children of Israel took over his land.

Then the people came to the border of one of the strongest nations of all, the nation of Moav.

Balaam The Prophet בלק

Balak was the king of Moav. He and his people were sure that the Children of Israel would attack and destroy Moav, and they were afraid.

The king gathered his wise men and the wise men of the neighboring nation, Midyan, and told them to go to Balaam the Prophet.

The wise men came to Balaam with gifts, and said, "Balak asks that you return with us. He wants you to curse the Children of Israel, for they cover the earth, they are so many. They are too powerful for us. He knows that whomever you bless is blessed and whomever you curse is cursed."

Balaam told the wise men to wait until morning. God would tell him what to do during the night.

That night, God told Balaam not to go with the wise men.

In the morning, Balaam told them he could not go.

The wise men returned to Balak with Balaam's answer. But Balak kept sending more and more important people to Balaam to get him to change his mind.

Finally, God told Balaam that he could go to Balak. "But you can only do what I tell you," God warned.

The Talking Donkey

Balaam saddled his donkey and began the journey to Balak. Balaam thought that he could convince God to let him curse the Children of Israel. But he was wrong.

God was angry with Balaam. An angel holding a sword appeared in front of Balaam. But only Balaam's donkey saw it. To avoid the angel, the donkey went off the path and into a field which had a fence around it.

BLE STORIES

Balaam began hitting the donkey to get it to return to the path. He could not see the angel that kept moving in front of them. The donkey kept trying to avoid the angel with the sword, and pressed Balaam's leg into the fence. Balaam hit the donkey even harder.

Finally, the angel stood in a narrow place where the donkey could not get around it. The donkey sat down, and Balaam kept hitting it with his staff. God made the donkey speak.

"What did I do to you that you hit me so much?" pleaded the donkey.

"You didn't listen to me," Balaam answered. "If I had a sword I would kill you!"

"But I have been your donkey all your life," cried the donkey. "Did I ever do this before?"

"No," admitted Balaam.

Then God showed Balaam the angel, and Balaam was scared.

"If it had not been for your donkey, I would have killed you," said the angel.

"I have sinned," Balaam said. "If I'm doing the wrong thing then I will return to my home," he told the angel.

The angel told Balaam to go to Balak, but to remember that he must say only what God tells him.

Balak And Balaam

When Balaam reached Balak, he explained that he could not do anything but repeat what God would tell him.

But Balak did not pay any attention to Balaam's warning. He took Balaam to a high hill where the idol Baal was worshipped. From there they could see the camp of the Children of Israel.

"Curse them from here," Balak demanded.

"How can I curse them?" Balaam asked. "If God is not angry with them, I have no power to curse them."

They moved to other high places. But each time Balaam opened his mouth to curse the Children of Israel, a blessing came out instead.

"How good are your tents, Children of Jacob. How good are your homes, Children of Israel," Balaam shouted. "The people will raise themselves like a lion and conquer any nation that stands in their way," he announced, although he really didn't want to.

Balak became very angry.

"I brought you here to curse my enemy, and all you do is bless them," he complained.

"But I told you," Balaam explained, "I can only say what God puts in my mouth."

Finally, Balaam went back home, and Balak returned to his city.

Idol Worship

The women of Moav and Midyan went to greet the Children of Israel. Soon, they talked many Jewish men into worshipping the idols of Moav and Midyan. They even convinced some of the men to leave their families and come live with them!

Moses had warned the people about idol worship. But they weren't listening. God told him that if any of the leaders of Israel were praying to idols, they had to be killed.

Just then, Zimri, a leader of the Tribe of Shimon, started praying to idols with a woman from Midyan, in front of everyone.

A plague broke out among the Children of Israel. Many of those who prayed to idols died during the plague.

Pinchas Saves The People פינחס

Pinchas was the son of Elazar, the Kohen Gadol. When he saw what Zimri and the woman from Midyan were doing, he took a spear and killed them both.

At that very moment, the plague that had killed so many people stopped.

God told Moses, "Pinchas stopped my anger. Because of him no more people will be harmed. He deserves a medal of Peace. My blessing for him is that his descendants will always be Kohanim."

Counting The People

After the plague, God told Moses and Elazar to count the people so that they would know how many were left.

All the men who were 20 years and older were counted. The total number of men was 601,730. The Levites were counted separately. Every Levite boy who was one month or older was counted. The total number of male Levites was 23,000.

The Daughters Of Zelafchad

The five daughters of Zelafchad came to Moses, Elazar, and the leaders of the people, and said, "Our father died in the desert and left behind no son to inherit his land. We want to inherit his land."

Moses asked God what to do.

"The daughters of Zelafchad are right," God told him. "Give them their father's land. And tell the people that if a man dies and has no son, then his land becomes the property of his daughters."

Moses Appoints Joshua

God told Moses that soon he would have to die.

"You will go up the mountain of Avarim and look at the Land that I will give the Children of Israel. But, because you didn't listen to me and you hit the rock, you cannot enter the Land."

Moses said to God, "Who will lead the people when I am gone? Don't let them be like sheep wandering around without a shepherd."

God explained that Joshua, Moses' helper, would be the new leader. Moses was to place him in front of Elazar the Kohen Gadol and in front of the people.

"You will put your hands on him," God commanded, "and give him some of the energy you have in you. Then the people will know he is the new leader and listen to him."

The Festival Sacrifices

Besides the two daily sacrifices that had to be brought in the mishkan, God told Moses about all the festival sacrifices the people had to bring.

There was a sacrifice that had to be brought on Shabbat, and another on the New Moon.

Each day of the seven days of Passover, sacrifices had to be brought. On the first and seventh day of Passover no work was allowed to be done by the people.

On Shavuot a sacrifice had to be brought, and no work was allowed to be done by the people. On Rosh Hashanah and Yom Kippur a sacrifice had to be brought too, and no work could be done.

All seven days of Sukkot, sacrifices had to be brought. No work could be done on the first day. Shemini Atzeret was celebrated eight days after Sukkot began. A sacrifice had to be brought, and no work could be done.

Making A Promise To God   מטות

If a man promises or swears to do something or to keep away from something, he must keep his word. Whatever comes out of his mouth, he must do.

The Battle Against Midyan

God told Moses to attack Midyan. They had brought idol worship to the Children of Israel, and that was a terrible thing to do. Pinchas took an army of 12,000 men, sounded the trumpets, and attacked Midyan. They destroyed all the idol worshippers.

When the army returned, Moses had them divide in half everything that they had taken from the people of Midyan. The army kept one half, and the other half was divided among the rest of the people.

The army gave some of what they captured to the Kohanim. The people gave some of what they received to the Levites.

How Cooking Utensils Become Kosher

Many soldiers brought back plates and pots and pans from the homes of the people of Midyan. These utensils were made of either gold, silver, copper, iron, tin, or lead. Since utensils used to cook or serve in may have had non-kosher food in them, the Children of Israel couldn't eat from these utensils until they did the following:

If the utensil had been used for broiling non-kosher food, the utensil had to be heated with fire until it became white hot. That way, anything non-kosher would be burned out of it.

If the utensil had been used for boiling non-kosher food, it had to be filled with water and heated until the water boiled over.

Two And One Half Tribes Settle Down

The Tribe of Reuven, the Tribe of Gad, and half the Tribe of Menashe liked the land of the Amorites, the land of Sihon and Og. They had a lot of cattle and sheep, and this was good grazing land.

So, they asked Moses if they could stay in the land and not cross over the Jordan river to the Land of Israel.

Moses said to them: "Do you think it is fair that the other tribes will have to do all the fighting when they come to Israel, while you stay here? When they see you living quietly here, the other tribes won't want to go on. You're behaving just like the spies who tried to prevent the people from going to the Land of Israel. Remember what happened to them and to all the people who listened to them!"

The leaders of the tribes of Gad and Reuven explained what they meant. "We will just leave our families and our cattle here," they said. "But we will go with you to the Land of Israel to fight with the other tribes."

Moses was happy with this answer, and he helped them settle their families in the cities that had once belonged to the Amorites.

Sending The Canaanites מסעי Away

In the fortieth year of their wandering through the desert, Moses wrote down all the 42 stops they had made since they left Egypt. God told Moses to tell the people that when they cross the Jordan River into the Land of Israel, they must send away all the Canaanite people who live there. The Canaanites were idol worshippers and all their idols had to be destroyed.

"If you don't drive out the Canaanites," God said, "they will drive you out."

The Borders Of The Land Of Israel

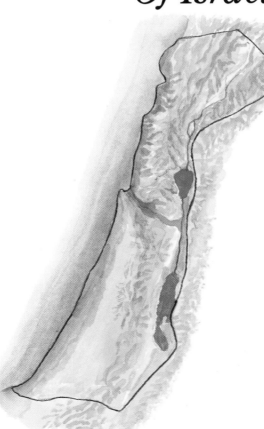

In order to divide the land among the nine-and-a-half tribes that did not have land yet, God told the people what the borders of the Land of Israel were to be.

Southern Border – The Desert of Zin, the edge of the Dead Sea, Atzmon, the Mediterranean Sea.

Northern Border – The Mediterranean Sea, Mount Hor, Zedad, Hazarenan.

Eastern Border – Hazarenan, Riblah, the Kinneret, the Jordan River, the Dead Sea.

Western Border – The Mediterranean Sea.

Cities Of Refuge

When the Children of Israel entered the Land they would have to build cities for the Levites. Altogether 48 cities for Levites would have to be built. Each tribe was to give some of its land to build the cities.

But six cities of the Levites were to be Cities of Refuge. Three of the Cities of Refuge were on the east side of the Jordan River where Reuven, Gad, and half the tribe of Menashe lived. The other three cities were to be used by the nine-and-a-half tribes.

God explained that "these six Cities of Refuge are for anyone who kills a person by accident."

If a person killed someone by accident, he could run to one of these six cities and he would be safe. No one who wanted to get back at him for what he did could hurt him. He would have to live in the city until the Kohen Gadol died. Then he could go home.

Living In Israel

God told Moses to tell the people that they have to conquer the Land of Israel. Once they did that, the entire land would be divided into 12 portions. The tribes with more people would receive more land than the tribes with fewer people.

In this way, all the families in the tribes would receive an equal portion.

MIDRASHIM
TALES OF OUR SAGES

במדבר

Why did the Tribe of Levi have the least amount of people?

It seems that the Tribe of Levi was excluded by Pharaoh from working as slaves. But Pharaoh made all the other tribes work hard, night and day. He felt sure that if they worked all the time, they would not have children, and soon the Jewish people would disappear. When God saw how hard the other tribes were working, God made them multiply. The more Pharaoh worked them the more children they had.

But since the Levites had not worked hard as slaves, they were not blessed with many children. That's why, while the smallest tribe had 32,000 people, the Tribe of Levi had only 22,000!

נשא

Why were the princes of each tribe the first ones to bring gifts for the dedication of the mishkan?

When God told Moses to ask the people for gold, silver, and other precious items to build the mishkan, the princes sat back and waited for the people to run out of valuable things to give. They were sure that Moses would then come to them and say, "Please give us what we're missing." The princes would of course give what was needed, and they would look like heroes.

As it turned out, however, the people gave even more than was needed. There was no need for the princes' gold, silver, and other valuables.

So this time, when there was a call to bring sacrifices to celebrate the dedication of the mishkan, the Princes were the first in line!

The Midrash explains the three blessings that the Kohanim give to the people as follows:

"May God bless you and keep you safe," deals with monetary matters. It means that God should bless you with prosperity and keep robbers from taking your wealth from you.

"May God's countenance shine upon you and may God be gracious to you," means that God should give you Torah knowledge and the wisdom to put this knowledge to good use.

"May God's countenance be turned to you and may God bring you peace," indicates that even when you sin against God, God's countenance continues to rest with you. But if you sin against your fellow man, that only your fellow man can forgive.

The idea of bringing peace is pivotal to the fulfillment of all the blessings, because without peace between man and man, wealth and wisdom are meaningless.

בהעלותך

After we read about the sacrifices brought by the princes, we are told about the menorah, which was lit by Aaron, the Kohen Gadol. What is the connection between these two sections?

The Midrash tells us that Aaron was upset when he saw that all the other tribes had brought offerings for the dedication of the mishkan. Only the Tribe of Levi, which includes the Kohanim, was not told to bring sacrifices.

"It is my fault," he thought. "It is because I made the Golden Calf that now my tribe, the Levites, will not be allowed to bring an offering."

God told Moses, "Tell your brother Aaron not to feel sad. His tribe will have the honor of taking part in a different dedication many years in the future."

That's exactly what happened. When the Greeks tried to destroy the Jewish people, the Maccabees, a family of Kohanim, defeated the Greek army and re-dedicated the Temple. They lit the flames of the menorah in the Temple, and because of this, Jews light Hanukkah menorahs all around the world.

In a way, Aaron's descendants' job was even greater than bringing sacrifices to the mishkan. After all, sacrifices were brought only when the Temple was standing, but Hanukkah menorahs are lit in every generation.

שלח

Why does this section begin with the words of God to Moses, "Send for yourself spies"? Moses certainly was not sending out the spies to please himself.

The Kli Yakar says that God was prophetically saying, "Send out the spies so that you – Moses – will live."

Moses was doomed to die in the desert because he hit the rock. Had the people entered the Land of Israel right away, he would have died at once. By sending the spies he inadvertently received a 40-year reprieve, because he continued to lead the Children of Israel in the desert.

The episode of the spies took place right after the story of Miriam and the story of Korach. But in the Torah, the story of the spies, found in Shelach, comes after the story of Miriam, but before the story of Korach. Why did the Torah change the order?

The Midrash explains that the Torah wants us to see what a terrible thing the spies did. A few days before they went on their mission they saw that Miriam had been punished for speaking badly about her brother, Moses. They should have learned a lesson from this. Speaking evil is a terrible sin. But even after seeing how

God gave her a terrible skin disease and how she was sent out of the camp, they still returned with an evil report about the Land of Israel.

Moses changed Joshua's name right before he left with the spies to the Land of Israel. He added a "yud" (which stands for God) to Joshua's name. Whenever Joshua thought about his new name, he remembered that God was always with him. In this way, he was able to withstand the pressure of the other spies who wanted him to speak badly about Israel.

When the people heard the news about the Land of Israel from the spies, they cried. They were sure that God was leading them to their deaths. But actually, they cried for nothing. God was only showing them how they could win, even against great odds.

However, because they cried for nothing that evening, God said, "I will make this night into a time of crying throughout your history."

The night they cried was the ninth of Av, Tisha B'Av – the day both the First Temple and the Second Temple were destroyed. And on this day many other tragedies occurred to the Jewish people as well.

God told Moses, after the sin of the spies, that "All those who have tested Me these ten times and not believed in Me will not enter the Land."

What were those ten tests?

1. When the Children of Israel saw the Egyptians chasing them at the sea, they said it would have been better to remain slaves in Egypt.
2. When they complained that they had nothing to drink except for the bitter waters.
3. When they ran out of food and complained.
4. When they saved manna, even though they were told not to.
5. When they went out to collect manna on Shabbat even though they were told not to.
6. When their water ran out, and they complained.
7. When they worshipped the Golden Calf.
8. When they rebelled against God's commandments and wanted to return to Egypt.
9. When they complained about the manna.
10. When they believed the spies' report about the Land of Israel.

Why were the Children of Israel given the mitzvah of tzitzit?

The Midrash says that tzitzit are like a royal uniform. They remind the one who wears them that he is always a servant of the king, and should behave as such.

קרח

What does the name Korach mean?

The root of the Hebrew word *Korach* means "bald." The Midrash says that Korach made the Jewish people bald by convincing many people to follow him. Figuratively speaking, he cut off the highest caliber of the Jewish people. In the end all these people died.

Korach tried to show the people that what Moses was telling them was illogical. He claimed Moses made things up. One of his arguments was as follows:

A mezuzah has parchment in it. On the parchment are passages from the Torah. Moses told the people that a mezuzah should be placed on the doorposts of a house as a form of protection for that house.

Korach asked, "If a mezuzah which has some passages of the Torah on it, protects a house, a house which is filled with books of the Torah certainly wouldn't need a mezuzah, now would it?"

In the Torah, we read that Ohn, the son of Pelet, also joined the rebellion against Moses. However, while he is listed as one of the rebels, we read nothing about him during the actual rebellion.

The Midrash says that Ohn's wife talked him out of staying with Korach's group. She said, "What can you possibly gain from joining Korach? Even if he is right and Moses is a dictator who only wants the glory of leadership, how will that benefit you? If Korach wins, then he will be in charge. Since you are not a Levite, you will still be where you are now. If Moses wins, then he will continue to lead, and you will have gained nothing – worse, you and I and all our family will most likely be punished."

Ohn agreed with her wise words and quickly left Korach and his cohorts. He, of all those who had initially rebelled, survived.

חקת

Perhaps the decree of the Red Cow came to atone for the sin of the Golden Calf. Just as a mother comes to clean up the mess made by her child, this cow cleanses the Children of Israel from the sin of the Golden Calf.

God helped the Children of Israel survive in the desert by giving them manna, water, and the pillars of cloud and fire.

According to the Midrash, the manna fell because of the merit of Moses; the Clouds of Glory led the people because of the merit of Aaron; and the well of water accompanied them because of the merit of Miriam.

Why was the well due to the merit of Miriam? This water was a reward because Miriam had waited at the banks of the Nile River to see what would happen to Moses.

But when Miriam died, the water dried up, and the people began to complain of thirst.

The commentator, Alsheich, adds that the well dried up because the people did not weep over Miriam's death as they did over the death of Aaron. They acted as though her death did not matter to them.

The Rambam explains that hitting the rock was not the real sin of Moses. Letting his anger get the best of him and calling the people "rebels" was his real sin. After all, the Children of Israel felt that Moses was reflecting God's will; if Moses was angry, it meant that God was angry as well. Yet, nowhere does the text indicate that God was angry at the people for complaining about the lack of water.

Similarly, Rashi tells us that Moses should have spoken to the rock, but the people's incessant complaints made him so angry that he lost his self-control and hit the rock. No leader of the Jewish people can afford the luxury of losing his self-control, especially a leader like Moses.

Why was Moses punished for hitting the rock when earlier, in the Parsha of B'shalach, after they left Egypt, Moses hit the rock, and God was not angry with him?

According to the commentator, Kli Yakar, the first time Moses went to get water from a rock he took only the Elders with him. They understood that it was God and not Moses or his staff that was drawing water from the rock.

But the second time, when Moses hit the rock, all the people were watching. They knew that Moses had done wonders in Egypt and even after that with his staff.

They began to think that perhaps the staff had some magic power in it. That's why God told Moses only to lift his staff, but not to hit the rock.

When Moses hit the rock with the staff and water poured out, he reinforced their belief in the power of the staff. This was a grave error.

Why were snakes used to punish the people?

Just as the first snake spoke against God to Eve, so too the Childre[n] of Israel spoke out against the manna that God sent to feed them. It was only fitting that the snake who was punished by not being able t[o] taste its food, should come and punish the people for being ungratef[ul] about the manna, the miraculous food of many flavors that God provided for them in the desert.

When the people looked up at the snake on the pole that Moses se[t] up, they were cured because they understood that their sin was just like the sin of the snake, and they repented.

The snake on a pole has become a very famous symbol of healing from Biblical time onward. It is known as the Caduceus, and it is th[e] symbol of medicine throughout the world today.

בלק

Why was Balaam given such prophetic powers?

The Midrash says that God did not want the other nations of the world to be able to say, "Had You given us a prophet like Moses, we would have been obedient to Your Will as well."

Now they had their prophet. But what did he use his gift of prophecy for? To try and counter God's Will and curse the Children of Israel.

God changed Balaam's curses into blessings. Many of these blessings have found their way into our daily prayers. This is to teac[h] us that the Children of Israel cannot be harmed against God's will.

The mishnah in Pirkay Avot tells us that Balaam's talking donkey was one of the things created just before the first Shabbat, after the six days of creation.

They included:

1. The donkey that spoke to Balaam.
2. The manna that the Israelites ate in the desert.
3. The staff that Moses carried and used to bring the 10 plagues and split the Red Sea.
4. The mouth of the earth that opened up and swallowed Korach and his followers.
5. The rainbow.
6. The shamir, the worm which could split rocks, and which King Solomon used to help carve the rocks for the Temple.
7. The Hebrew letters, and the words that were engraved in the Tablets of Law. They could be read from all directions.

8. The first Tablets of Law.
9. The ram that Abraham used as a sacrifice instead of offering Isaac.
10. Miriam's well which traveled with the Children of Israel in the desert.

Why was Balaam's donkey given the power of speech?

In order to show Balaam that even the power to speak is under God's control. If God could make an animal speak intelligently, then surely Balaam could be forced to say the words that God wanted him to say.

The Kli Yakar adds that just as the donkey had been given the power of speech only to glorify the Children of Israel, so too Balaam was given the power of prophecy for the same reason – and not because he deserved it!

פינחס

How is it that God gave Pinchas the blessing of Peace after he killed a prince of Israel?

The Midrash answers this question with a story:

A king was traveling on a road with his soldiers when he came across a group of men. One of them insulted the king, and the king was ready to kill them all. Suddenly, a member of the group turned and killed the man who had insulted the king. When the king saw that there was a righteous man among the group, his anger abated, and he decided to spare them all.

God was angry with the Children of Israel for their immoral behavior, especially for the fact that no one corrected this sinful behavior. But when Pinchas risked his life and killed Zimri in order to sanctify the Name of God, then, like the king in the story, God turned anger into praise for Pinchas.

Prior to Pinchas' actions, only newborn children of Aaron's family were to become Kohanim. Anyone born before the dedication of the mishkan was not to become a Kohen. But when Pinchas acted so zealously, God declared Pinchas and his descendants Kohanim too.

In reviewing those who were counted by Moses and Aaron, the Torah says, "And these men were counted but would not go into the Land." This was the generation that was counted from the age of 20 years in the desert and destined to die in the desert.

But what about the women?

Rashi tells us that the women loved the Land. So while the men were saying, "Let's go back to Egypt!" the women, like the daughters of Zelafchad were saying, "give us a portion in the Land of Israel."

מטות

When the two-and-a-half tribes came to ask Moses to remain on the eastern side of the Jordan River, they said, "Let us just build pens for our flocks and our livestock and cities for our children, and then we'll go with you to fight with the other tribes."

But when Moses permitted their request, he reversed the order and said, "Build cities for your children and pens for your flocks." Moses wanted them to understand Jewish priorities: First comes family, and then flocks, cattle, and everything else.

מסעי

Why does this section have a review of all the places the Children of Israel stopped during their 40 years of wandering?

Rashi explains that mentioning the 42 encampments of the Children of Israel was the Torah's way of telling us that there was actually very little "wandering" that the Jewish people had to do during the 40 years.

In fact, while they moved through the desert 14 times during the first year, and 8 times during the last year, they moved only 20 times during the middle 38 years! Most of their years in the desert were spent without wandering or traveling.

God commanded Moses to tell the people to set up six Cities of Refuge, three on the eastern side of the Jordan River, but only three on the western side of the Jordan, where most of the tribes would be living. Shouldn't the number of cities on the western side of the Jordan River have been at least double that of the eastern side?

Rashi points out that on the eastern side of the Jordan River there was the city of Gilad belonging to the Tribe of Menashe. This city had many murderers in it. So, even though this area had less people than the western bank of the Jordan River, they needed the same amount of cities as the rest of Israel.

The six Cities of Refuge were not functional until all six were completed. Nevertheless, we find that Moses immediately began to build three cities on his side – the eastern side – of the Jordan. He certainly knew they could not be used until the other three cities were built. So why didn't Moses leave the building of these cities to Joshua and those who would conquer the Land of Israel?

We learn from this that when you have a commandment you should perform it even if you won't be able to finish it. The act of doing the commandment is a mitzvah in itself.

THE BOOK OF RUTH

THE BOOK OF RUTH is the story of Ruth's journey to become part of the Jewish people.

THE BOOK OF RUTH is read on the holiday of Shavuot. On Shavuot, God gave the Jewish people the Ten Commandments. When they were asked whether they wanted the Torah, the Jewish people shouted "We will do the commandments and we will listen to them!"

any years ago, in the Land of Israel, there was a famine. The seeds the farmers planted did not grow, and there was little water to be found.

In the town of Bethlehem there lived a man named Elimelech, his wife Naomi, and their two sons, Machlon and Kilion. They lived on a big farm. When Elimelech saw that the crops wouldn't grow, and that the water had dried up, he took his family to Moav, a country near Israel. There he bought a piece of land and started farming again.

Elimelech died, and his two sons married women from Moav. They were called Ruth and Orpah.

After about 10 years, Machlon and Kilion died. Naomi heard that God had sent rain to the Land of Israel, and that the crops were growing again. So, together with her daughters-in-law, Ruth and Orpah, Naomi set off for Bethlehem.

On the way, Naomi told her daughters-in-law to return to their parents' houses. "Thank you," she said, "for being so nice to me and my sons. But now you should leave me. I hope that God takes good care of you."

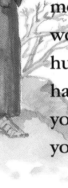

Naomi kissed Ruth and Orpah, and the two girls cried. "We can't leave you," they wailed. "We want to go with you."

"But you can't come with me," Naomi explained. "You won't be able to find husbands in Israel, and I have no more children for you to marry. Go back to your homes."

The two girls cried some more. Then Orpah kissed

her mother-in-law and went back to her parents' house. But Ruth wouldn't go.

"Look at your sister-in-law," Naomi said. "She's going back to her family. Follow her example."

But Ruth wouldn't budge. "Please don't make me go," she pleaded. "Wherever you go, I want to go. Wherever you live, I want to live. Your people will be my people. Your God will be my God. And when you're old and die, I want to be buried right near you. I want to be near you always."

When Naomi saw how much Ruth wanted to stay with her, she shrugged and continued walking to Bethlehem. Ruth stayed by her side and helped her during the difficult journey.

When Naomi arrived in Bethlehem, everyone she had known was amazed at how old she looked.

"My life has been bitter," Naomi complained. "That's why I look like I do. Call me Bitterness, not Naomi. God has punished me for leaving Israel, and I have lost everything."

Naomi and Ruth stayed on the farm of Elimelech. But it was rundown and there was nothing to eat. So, Ruth went out to find food. It was the time of the barley harvest, and as always, Jewish farmers left a little bit of their harvest for the poor people to take. Ruth went from field to field to see what she could find.

She ended up in the field of a man named Boaz. When Boaz found out who she was, he went over to her.

"I have heard about you," Boaz told her. "I have heard how you take care of Naomi. I pray that God will reward you for your actions. Please don't go to any other fields. You will find enough here for you and your mother-in-law."

"Thank you," Ruth answered. "You have made me feel very good."

Boaz told his servants to secretly put out some extra barley sheaves for Ruth to pick up.

When Ruth returned to her mother-in-law, she showed her all the barley she had taken from the field of Boaz. It

was enough to feed them for many days.

"Where did you get all this?" asked Naomi. "I gathered all this in the field of a man named Boaz," Ruth told her.

"Boaz!" Naomi exclaimed. "Why, the man is a relative of ours," she told Ruth. "He is someone who can help us."

When the harvest was completed, everyone met at the granary for a harvest party. Naomi told Ruth to dress in her finest clothing and stay close to Boaz. He would tell her what to do.

At the harvest party, Ruth went over to Boaz and thanked him for taking care of her.

As she talked, Boaz realized that Ruth was filled with kindness and concern for others.

"I know I am much older than you, but I want you to marry me," Boaz told Ruth. "And if I could, I would marry you right now. But there is someone who is an even closer relative than I. By the custom of our people, he has a chance to marry you first."

The next day, Boaz gathered the wise men of the city. Then he brought Ploni Almoni, the closest relative of Elimelech, to the wise men.

"Sir," he said to Ploni Almoni, "the land that belonged to our relative Elimelech is up for sale. If you

want to buy it, please let us know."

"I will be glad to buy it," said Ploni Almoni.

"But, if you buy the land," continued Boaz, "you must also marry Ruth, the woman from Moav. She was married to one of Elimelech's children, and it is only right that you marry her. That way, when you two have children, you can name them after Elimelech and his children."

"That, I don't want to do!" snapped Ploni Almoni. "I'm not marrying anyone from Moav. My family has never married anyone outside of Israel. Look, Boaz, you're a relative too. Why don't you marry her and take the land?"

"That's exactly what I'll do!" Boaz said, smiling.

Now, as was the custom in those days when selling land, Ploni Almoni took off his shoe and gave it to Boaz. But not for keeps. Boaz then gave him back the shoe.

Now the land, and Ruth, belonged to Boaz.

Everyone cheered! They were happy that Boaz would have a wonderful wife like Ruth.

And so, Boaz married Ruth. They had a son called Oved. Naomi took care of Oved and enjoyed her grandson.

Oved was to become the father of Yishai. And Yishai was the father of David, the famous King of Israel.